EMERALD TABLET SIX THE KEY OF MAGIC

A Channeled Revelation from

Thoth The Atlantean

Rebecca Marina Messenger

Format Copyright 2024 by Rebecca Marina Messenger
All rights reserved.

No part of this publication may be reproduced, distributed, or transmitted in any form or by any means, including photocopying, recording, or other electronic or mechanical methods, without the prior written permission of the publisher, except in the case of brief quotations embodied in critical reviews and certain other noncommercial uses permitted by copyright law. For permission requests, email the publisher at Rebecca@rebeccamarina.com

ISBN: (E-Book) ISBN: 978-1-7374211-2-2

ISBN: (Print) ISBN: 978-1-7374211-3-9

Additional Resources to support you:

Just to thank you for reading my book, I'd love to share these gifts that have transformed my life, AND deepened my Spiritual abilities. Now, I'm excited to pass them on to you.

Three Powerful Free Gifts!

Bonus #1. Free Mini-Course: <u>Three Ways to Attract More Money, Love, and Joy – Starting NOW!</u> Instantly unlock Abundance, Love, and Happiness with these proven techniques.

Bonus #2: Three Secrets to Instantly Boost Your Healing Powers
Supercharge your healing abilities with these simple, effective methods.

Bonus #3: Atlantean Power Words
Accelerate your Chakra System and repel unwanted energies using little-known Sacred words from ancient Atlantis.

Free at: https://www.eftexpert.com/

PROLOGUE

When Thoth the Atlantean first asked me to "channel His guidance" for Emerald Tablet Six... I resisted.

Emerald Tablet Six, *The Key of Magic*, to me, has always felt like the most challenging Tablet to grasp. Yet, deep down, I knew that if I simply sat down and allowed Thoth's words to flow through me, the process would unfold naturally. And that's exactly what happened.

I began by placing all the verses of Tablet Six into a document. One by one, I left space beneath each verse, waiting for Thoth to illuminate its meaning in today's language. His intention was clear: the ancient wisdom should be accessible, and easily understood by modern readers.

You may notice, though, that even in "plain language," some of the words still carry an old-fashioned flair - which is fitting, considering that Thoth the Atlantean is over 35,000 years old!

As you read, I invite you to move through each verse slowly, allowing the deeper layers of meaning to reveal themselves. At the end of each chapter, you'll find a blank page - space for your thoughts, reflections, and questions. Thoth welcomes your inquiries, and you may be surprised at the ways in which the answers will find their way to you.

One more thing: Thoth shared with me that His symbol is the dragonfly. Don't be surprised if you begin to notice dragonflies appearing in your life. The dragonfly spends years in water, undergoing various stages of transformation before emerging as the graceful winged creature we see. Like the dragonfly, we too undergo deep, unseen transformations as we ascend into higher levels of consciousness.

OTHER BOOKS BY REBECCA MARINA MESSENGER:

1. <u>Study Edition: The Emerald Tablets of Thoth The Atlantean -</u> Available from Amazon, Barnes and Noble, and other Fine Bookstores
2. The Secret Key to The Emerald Tablets: Revealed by Thoth The Atlantean With His Divine Feminine Counterpart - Available at all Bookstores
3. The Pleiadian Protocol for Reducing Excess Body Mass in Humans: The Never Before Revealed Secret Science from the Stars - Available on Amazon.com
4. Spiritually Decalcify the Pineal Gland - Available on Amazon.com
5. Cure White Sugar and Chocolate Cravings in One Hour: The Simple Secret You Need for Effortless Automatic Control Over Your Cravings - Available on Amazon.com
6. Book of Comfort 1: How the Earth Began, The Origin of Miracles, and a New Connection with Holy Spirit (Book of Comfort, The Messenger Series) Available on Amazon.com

DEDICATION

This book is dedicated to all of those who seek to understand The Emerald Tablets.

I am grateful to my wonderful husband, Thomas, and to my family. I am especially grateful to my "Eagle Eyes" editor… Lee K. Wolf!

TABLE OF CONTENTS

Chapter One: Tablet 6, Verse 1. Forgotten Powers/
    Eternal Struggle 1

Chapter Two: Tablet 6, Verse 2. The Eternal Struggle
    of Darkness. 4

Chapter Three: Tablet 6, Verse 3. The Suns of Morning's
    Descent 6

Chapter Four: Tablet 6, Verse 4. Feebly Flamed
    the Light 9

Chapter Five: Tablet 6, Verse 5. Fetters of the Night 12

Chapter Six: Tablet 6, Verse 6. Secret Enslavers
    of Souls. 15

Chapter Seven: Tablet 6, Verse 7. The Seduction
    of Power 19

Chapter Eight: Tablet 6, Verse 8. Dreamwalkers
    of Darkness 22

Chapter Nine: Tablet 6, Verse 9. Breaking the Veil
    of Night. 25

Chapter Ten: Tablet 6, Verse 10. The Pursuit of Light's
    Pathway 28

Chapter Eleven: Tablet 6, Verse 11. Weigh the Words
    of Light 34

Chapter Twelve: Tablet 6, Verse 12. Conqueror
of Darkness 37

Chapter Thirteen: Tablet 6, Verse 13. Light Rends the Veil
of Darkness 41

Chapter Fourteen: Tablet 6, Verse 14. Guides of
the Eternal Way. 47

Chapter Fifteen: Tablet 6, Verse 15. Eternal Victory
of Light 54

Chapter Sixteen: Tablet 6, Verse 16. Lords of the
Morning Sun .57

Chapter Seventeen: Tablet 6, Verse 17. Paths of the
Unbound Master. 61

Chapter Eighteen: Tablet 6, Verse 18. Conquering the
Phantom of Fear 64

Chapter Nineteen: Tablet 6, Verse 19. The Battle Within
the Mind. 67

Chapter Twenty: Tablet 6, Verse 20. The Conquering
Wisdom 71

Chapter Twenty-one: Tablet 6, Verse 21. Guarding the
Mind's Gate. 73

Chapter Twenty-two: Tablet 6, Verse 22. The Power
of Knowing. 77

Chapter Twenty-three: Tablet 6, Verse 23. Ritual of
Liberation. .80

Chapter Twenty-four: Tablet 6, Verse 24. Chant of the
Seven Lords 83

Chapter Twenty-five: Tablet 6, Verse 25. The Power of
                    Sacred Names. 86

Chapter Twenty-six: Tablet 6, Verse 26. Lift Thy Brother
                    from Night 89

Chapter Twenty-seven: Tablet 6, Verse 27. Ascend with
                    My Words. 92

Chapter Twenty-eight: Tablet 6, Verse 28. The Path of
                    Peace and Power 94

Chapter Twenty-nine: Final Thoughts 97

Chapter Thirty: About the Author 99

EMERALD TABLET SIX: THE KEY OF MAGIC

A Channeled Revelation from Thoth the Atlantean

From the Author: Through direct channeling from Thoth the Atlantean, I have translated the profound Wisdom of Emerald Tablet Six into clear, present-day language. What was once most difficult to comprehend, is now accessible and usable for all.

At the end of each Chapter, a blank page is provided for your notes and questions. Writing down your questions invites the Universe's attention, and you may be pleasantly surprised by how the answers reveal themselves in unexpected ways.

Chapter One

TABLET 6, VERSE 1. FORGOTTEN POWERS/ETERNAL STRUGGLE

Hark ye, O man, to the wisdom of magic.
Hark to the knowledge of powers forgotten.

Long, long ago in the days of the first man,
warfare began between darkness and light.

Men, then as now,
were filled with both darkness and light;
and while in some, darkness held sway,
in others, light filled the soul.

Thoth's Insight in Plain Language:

It is time for humanity to rekindle the proper and good use of Magic. Much good can be brought about by remembering the old ways. You have the knowledge of Magic deep within your cellular memories.

For too long has the power of darkness held sway over man. As more and more of you remember your birthright… new forms of Magic shall arise.

You were born to embrace the Light.

It is only through the turning away from the Light, that much sorrow has covered the Earth. This is a time of great calamity, and YOU are being called to set it right!

As you accept the guidance found within these pages, you will find yourself a very great instrument in turning the tide to the right.
Yes! It is not by chance that you are reading these words. Even as you read, my energy is awakening secrets within you!

Fear not! You will never be asked to do more than you are capable of doing.

NOTES AND QUESTIONS

Chapter Two

TABLET 6, VERSE 2. THE ETERNAL STRUGGLE OF DARKNESS

Aye, age old is this warfare,
the eternal struggle between darkness and light.
Fiercely is it fought all through the ages,
using strange powers hidden to man.

Thoth's Insight in Plain Language:

Since time immemorial, has this struggle between Light and dark ensued. It is time now for more of humanity to place their awareness on the Light.

Now is the time for humanity to turn away from the false promises of power from the dark brothers.

You have a built-in compass to steer you ever and always toward the Light. Hearken to the messages in your heart. Do so… and you will never be deceived!

NOTES AND QUESTIONS

Chapter Three

TABLET 6, VERSE 3. THE SUNS OF MORNING'S DESCENT

Adepts have there been, filled with the blackness,
struggling always against the light;
but others there are who, filled with brightness,
have ever conquered the darkness of night.

Where e'er ye may be in all ages and planes,
surely ye shall know of the battle with night.

Long ages ago, the SUNS of the Morning,
descending, found the world filled with night.

There in that past time began the struggle,
the age old battle of darkness and Light.

Thoth's Insight in Plain Language:
Hold your tongue when speaking of those who are encompassed by darkness. For in the speaking of

it… there arises a fear in man, which feeds the fire of their wickedness.

Far better to always speak of Light, and the all-encompassing healing power of LOVE!

Yes, the Earth was once covered in darkness, until the Spirit of the Light moved upon the waters. This illuminated the good… yet still conflict arose. A shortcut to power, was the instigating emotion craved by those who resisted the Light.

There have always been those who paid heed to the calling and TRUTH within their hearts. They believe NOT the seduction of the dark powers. There is naught to fear, for total protection is found within the trust of the Light.

NOTES AND QUESTIONS

Chapter Four

TABLET 6, VERSE 4. FEEBLY FLAMED THE LIGHT

Many in that time were so filled with darkness that only feebly flamed the light from the night.

*Note from Rebecca: This is in line with something Sanat Kumara told me long ago: "At one time the flame in man's heart was almost extinguished. It was then that I intervened for the souls of all men."

Thoth's Insight in Plain Language:

At one time in the history of man, it seemed that all was lost to the darkness. Yet even the most feeble flame was enough to bring back the roar of the Inner Fire of the heart!

Even NOW, if people would pay attention to the GOOD, to the honorable… the reverence of the heart would be a soothing balm to bind up the wounds of those in pain.

Pain can come from feeling that one is fighting a losing battle against chaos. I say… rest in the love that you can pull from the wisdom of your heart.

One tiny ray of Light and Love, turned upon the dark, can cause the roar of heartfire to obliterate the dark.

What say you, brothers and sisters? Shall we together bring healing to this planet, by allowing our heart-love to wield the power of which it is capable?

NOTES AND QUESTIONS

Chapter Five

TABLET 6, VERSE 5. FETTERS OF THE NIGHT

Some there were, masters of darkness,
who sought to fill all with their darkness;
sought to draw others into their night.

Fiercely withstood they, the masters of brightness:
fiercely fought they from the darkness of night.

Sought they ever to tighten the fetters,
the chains that bind man to the darkness of night.

Used they always the dark magic,
brought into man by the power of darkness;
magic that enshrouded man's soul with darkness.

Thoth's Insight in Plain Language:
Those of the dark are ever seeking to bring about the downfall of man. They use any means at their

disposal, and as always, hesitate NOT to use the powers of dark Magic!

The greatest of these deceptions is the promise of greater power and wealth to those who choose to follow blindly, lured by these false promises.

Know this: No matter what the promise or enticement of the dark Magic, it can never overcome the Light!

The Light never gives up - even on those who seem to have turned their soul completely to the dark. This is one reason why it is best NOT to be always in fear of the dark.

Fear adds to the power of darkness over man. Realize that those perpetrating evil are always in the grip of dark Magic.

Imagine that a ray of Light from YOU, could be just what is needed to turn the heart away from the darkness, and leave the evil ways behind.

It is foolish to think that YOU have no power, my brothers and sisters… for even the tiniest ray of Light has far more power than you can imagine!

Be the one who is willing to transpose FEAR - and send out rays of kindness and Light.

NOTES AND QUESTIONS

Chapter Six

TABLET 6, VERSE 6. SECRET ENSLAVERS OF SOULS

Banded together in an order,
BROTHERS of DARKNESS,
they through the ages,
antagonists they to the children of men.

Walked they always secret and hidden,
found, yet not found, by the children of men.

Forever they walked and worked in darkness,
hiding from the light in the darkness of night.

Silently, secretly, use they their power,
enslaving and binding the souls of men.

Thoth's Insight in Plain Language:

This is still true, as there are many who are hiding in high places of influence. It might seem that they are so powerful that mankind does not have a chance to resist their power. Yet, you Beloved ones, DO have the power.

You have free will - and you have the most reliable compass that exists. A compass that cannot be corrupted if you know the value of it. I am speaking of the compass within your heart.

The key to resisting every temptation placed in your path by these dark ones, is to trust the inner whispers of your heart.

It is necessary to tune in physically to your heart. Imagine that your heart is a sentient being (it is). Give your heart full permission to guide you.

The heart is never confused… even if your mind is confused and tempted!

Meditation to trust your hearts Guidance: Find audio of this meditation at https://www.eftexpert.com/blog/meditation-to-trust-your-hearts-guidance

Meditation begins: Relax, and just know that all is well. Relax the muscles in your head, your neck, and your shoulders. The purpose of this meditation is to build up your faith and trust in your own beautiful heart.

For it is true, beloved, that all you need is already within you. Your purpose was planned even before you came into this physical incarnation. And all that you need is indeed already written on the walls of your heart.

So, as you close your eyes and you're being very relaxed, that relaxation is filtering down throughout your entire body. Your back relaxes, your chest relaxes, arms and hands relax. Isn't it good to be so very relaxed?

And now, bring your awareness to your heart, your physical beating heart, and place your hand on your heart to make that physical connection.

Now, imagine that a line of light is coming through your crown, throughout your cranial cavity, illuminating all the glands within your cranium.

It brings that light down to your physical beating heart. See that when that light comes into your heart, you can imagine that you can see your own heart flame.

That Heart Flame is fueled by pure Source energy. Then, as you put your awareness on your heart flame, and the connection it has with your thoughts originating in your brain, everything becomes clearer.

Imagine that you can see that flame in your heart just growing brighter and brighter as you allow yourself to trust, and this feeling of security washes over you.

You feel so peaceful, and you know that everything is going to be all right. You're going to be all right. Trust in your heart, and it is so. It is so. It is so.

NOTES AND QUESTIONS

Chapter Seven

TABLET 6, VERSE 7. THE SEDUCTION OF POWER

Unseen they come, and unseen they go.
Man, in his ignorance, calls THEM from below.

Thoth's Insight in Plain Language:

This is speaking of those humans, who are so eager for power, that they engage in Rituals that they believe are innocent. This is an innocent perpetration, they think. Yet, hidden in the Rituals, are powerful words and phrases, which are designed to awaken and summon evil shapeshifters for the destruction of man!

These shapeshifters would have no power - except for the power that greed gives them. Be always mindful of that… if you are offered a shortcut to power over others! This is a seduction of your soul.

Do not point your finger at others and say… "Oh, these people are in the grip of seduction." Instead, attend to your own heart, and do not give "voice-power" to others.

Where you place your attention grows in power! If you place your attention on evil with an emotion of fear… its power grows! Instead, place your attention on things, acts, and emotions of Love, kindness, and joy!

NOTES AND QUESTIONS

Chapter Eight

TABLET 6, VERSE 8.
DREAMWALKERS OF DARKNESS

Dark is the way the DARK BROTHERS travel,
dark with a darkness not of the night,
traveling o'er Earth
they walk through man's dreams.

Power have they gained
from the darkness around them
to call other dwellers from out of their plane,
in ways that are dark and unseen by man.

Into man's mind-space reach the DARK BROTHERS.
Around it, they close the veil of their night.

There through its lifetime
that soul dwells in bondage,
bound by the fetters of the VEIL of the night.

Mighty are they in the forbidden knowledge,
forbidden because it is one with the night.

Thoth's Insight in Plain Language:

Here, it is urgent NOT to allow these words to place you in a state of fear. At the time of this writing, there were many power-hungry men who participated in calling forth these evil, seducing shapeshifters.

These men would command these dark shapeshifters to go into the minds of those that they desired to sway toward darkness.

They would do rituals to send these energies into the dream states of those whom they desired to control.

There is no need to fear this at this time, if you continually tune your own heart to the Light! **The mind cannot override the power of a pure heart.**

Trust always your own heart. The Divine Light is there - and you have nothing to fear… ever!

However, if you have allowed your mind to slip a bit, and be turned to the possibility of improving your life by adhering to some of these ancient dark ways… cleanse yourself by making a firm decision to turn always to the Light!

The Light will always and forever be a permanent CURE for resisting the effects of darkness.

NOTES AND QUESTIONS

Chapter Nine

TABLET 6, VERSE 9.
BREAKING THE VEIL OF NIGHT

Hark ye, O man, and list to my warning:
be ye free from the bondage of night.

Surrender not your soul
to the BROTHERS OF DARKNESS.

Keep thy face ever turned toward the LIGHT.
Know ye not, O man, that your sorrow,
only has come through the Veil of the night.

Aye, man, heed ye my warning:
strive ever upward,
turn your soul toward the LIGHT.

Thoth's Insight in Plain Language:

Again and again, Light Beings sound the warning, and shall continue to be the reminding force in your ears. The only struggles which mankind has suffered, have been because of giving in to the suggestions and cunning stealth of the darker forces.

So very subtle can they be, that many are fooled. It seems that the dark brothers often present a new path that SEEMS to be the right one… yet it quickly veers away from the path of the Soul's Light.

It is important to stop, and assess where you are at every moment! If you have veered away from the path of Light, forgive yourself, and any others who may have tempted you.

The Light is ALWAYS waiting for you to choose the path back home! There is no judgment, for the Source of Light understands that you are growing through your experiences.

Often, it may be necessary for you to wake up and pay attention to exactly HOW you go to the place where you find yourself currently.

If you always tune into your heart, you will always be able to right yourself, and swerve to turn back to a higher path.

These words are meant to encourage you to TRUST that you DO have your own Source of Power within.

You do not need to gain power from outside sources. Trust in your own abilities to choose the way of Light! You can now, and have been, choosing the path of Light, throughout many lifetimes!

NOTES AND QUESTIONS

Chapter Ten

TABLET 6, VERSE 10. THE PURSUIT OF LIGHT'S PATHWAY

The BROTHERS of DARKNESS seek for their brothers those who have traveled the pathway of LIGHT.

For well know they that those who have traveled
far towards the Sun in their pathway of LIGHT
have great and yet greater power
to bind with darkness the children of LIGHT.

Thoth's Insight in Plain Language:

Yes, it is true that the brothers of darkness seek to convert those who have traveled the path of Light. They seek to overwhelm these Light brothers with temptations of greed, avarice, and any pretty bauble of lust which they can dangle in front of them. Like an insidious greed for the power of unearned wealth, the dark brothers seek to blind them.

They do this because they know that these new brothers will bring much power to their own darkness. To ones who have truly walked the path of Light, and felt the commitment in their heart... no amount of greed-based offering can sway them!

Still, the dark brothers ever seek to snare those who are susceptible, and who have one little chink in their armor of Light. To avoid being swallowed up by the temptations of greed, power, or lust... focus your life always on the true Christ-grid Light within your heart.

Whenever ANY new shiny object is presented to you as a temptation... simply check in with your heart Light! It is said that one cannot lie to that power known as the Holy Spirit of Highest Light!

Always seek to fill yourself with that Holy Spirit Light. This power has been known by many names throughout history. It is the INCORRUPTIBLE Light of Source!

Meditation to Cleanse and Activate with Three Powerful Streams of Holy Spirit Light: Listen to the audio on Rebecca's blog.
https://www.eftexpert.com/blog/holy-spirit-cleanse

Rebecca here - ready to guide you in a beautiful cleansing exercise.

This exercise uses one of the most powerful frequencies known, the power of Holy Spirit Light. We'll be working with three different streams of Holy Spirit light.

White Light of Holy Spirit:
Imagine the white robes of Christ or the white robes of a goddess, symbolizing beautiful purification.

Primary Colors Twisted Together:
The second stream combines the three primary colors twisted together, forming either black or a deep, deep purple… depending on the predominant color. Think of this stream as the darkness of the void, or the womb of creation. It possesses strong magnetic properties, attracting and removing energetic debris and obstructions as you allow the Holy water to do its work.

Clear Light of Holy Spirit:
The final stream, considered the most powerful, is clear Light. When it enters your body, it transforms into holy water, cleansing and expanding.

It's akin to a dried-up creek receiving a gully-washer of rain. It rapidly expands and conducts electricity and information, helping you to become more balanced as your body's electrical system becomes harmonized.

Close your eyes and listen to my voice, as you begin the relaxation process. Relax your head, neck, and shoulders. Take a deep, soft breath into your belly, letting it become soft. Feel the peaceful, loving sensation wash over you.

Let this relaxation flow down your entire body, from your back to the front, through your chest, abdomen, and down your legs, all the way to your feet. You're now floating on a soft, fluffy cloud.

Set the intention to be cleansed and purified by the incorruptible Light of the Holy Spirit.

Relaxing further, imagine your crown opening, allowing a pure white streak of Holy Spirit Light to flow through your cranial cavity, down your body, and into your heart. This soft white Light is filled with Love.

Now, shift your focus to your crown once more. The magnetic black Light of the Holy Spirit enters, attracting disruptive thoughts and cleansing them from your being.

Allow these particles to be drawn down to your perineum and then back up, dissolving them completely.

Now, envision something which you desire to have in your life, and send out this magnetic stream of Holy Spirit Light to effortlessly draw it to you.

Feel the presence, and the filling, of the Holy Spirit's Light.

Open your crown once more. Clear Holy Spirit Light enters… becoming holy water, purifying your entire being, and expanding your heart's capacity to Love and receive Love.

See yourself as the beautiful human that you are, surrounded by Divine Beings. They move in a circle, chanting ancient Blessings, and stretching forth their hands to bless you.

You're bathed in golden, healing, cleansing light… as if the gates of Heaven have opened.

Stay in this meditative space as long as you desire, knowing that you're loved and unique in your own way.

Thank you to the people at www.musicofwisdom.com for the beautiful meditation music. May they also be Blessed.

NOTES AND QUESTIONS

Chapter Eleven

TABLET 6, VERSE 11.
WEIGH THE WORDS OF LIGHT

List ye, O man, to he who comes to you.
But weigh in the balance if his words be of LIGHT.

For many there are who walk in DARK BRIGHTNESS and yet are not the children of LIGHT.

Thoth's Insight in Plain Language:

Increase your discernment by listening to those who come to you seeming to spout Wisdom! Yet, pass their words through the filter of your heart Light! For there are many who masquerade as Beings of the Light, in order to confuse and cause chaos!

Some are very adept at this masquerade game! In the times of Atlantis, when those practicing dark Magic would call up evil shape-shifters, these evil ones would take over the bodies and personalities of certain leaders in order to do harm.

This will NEVER happen to you - if you ALWAYS turn to the Wisdom within your own heart, and let not yourself be swayed by religious phenomena.

Beware of those who seek to demonstrate power by performing great feats of Magic, healing, or even sparks of Light from thin air!

Yes, it is possible that a Being of Light could do great wonders. Yet, ALWAYS let your heart be the judge! NEVER be taken in by signs and wonders, unless those are followed up and given in the spirit of service and Love.

There is ONLY ONE thing to trust - that is the never-failing compass within your heart!

Remember the example of that One called Christ when He was on earth. He did MANY miraculous healings and great works… yet he never boasted or even took credit.

He always pointed to that Source Power. According to the scriptures written of these miraculous acts… Christ is quoted as saying: "Greater things than this shall ye do!"

NOTES AND QUESTIONS

Chapter Twelve

TABLET 6, VERSE 12.
CONQUEROR OF DARKNESS

Easy it is to follow their pathway,
easy to follow the path that they lead.

But yet, O man, heed ye my warning:
Light comes only to him who strives.

Hard is the pathway that leads to the WISDOM,
hard is the pathway that leads to the LIGHT.

Many shall ye find, the stones in your pathway;
many the mountains to climb toward the LIGHT.

Yet know ye, O man, to him that o'ercometh,
free will he be of the pathway of Light.

Follow ye not the DARK BROTHERS ever.
Always be ye a child of the Light.

For know ye, O man,
in the end LIGHT must conquer
and darkness and night be banished from Light.

Thoth's Insight in Plain Language:

Far easier it would seem to just give in to the "easy way" of getting ahead… by choosing the path of greed, not caring for your fellow humans, and seeking only to serve yourself!

However; this is never a Soul-satisfying path. It may seem easier to get ahead in physical life by seeking only self-interest… This is the cunning path of darkness!

It may seem far more difficult to follow the path of Light… for it takes focus on the whole, rather than on one single part. Your heart seeks to always choose the path of Light! It is the only way to true Soul satisfaction!

For, in every human, was placed a homing beam to always seek Light! It takes a greater will to ignore that Light-seeking fragment, than to go wholeheartedly toward the darkness.

No one who serves the dark masters can ever be fully happy, because that Source-placed FRAGMENT can never be fully silenced!

Even at death, that Source-placed fragment will ever urge the heart to choose the Light! All is NEVER lost - for the Source keeps a record of every hair on your head, and seeks always to bring one home to the Light.

NOTES AND QUESTIONS

Chapter Thirteen

TABLET 6, VERSE 13.
LIGHT RENDS THE VEIL OF DARKNESS

Listen, O man, and heed ye this wisdom;
even as darkness, so is the LIGHT.

When darkness is banished and all Veils are rended, out there shall flash from the darkness, the LIGHT.

Thoth's Insight in Plain Language:
Soon, there will come a time of great reckoning! The wiles of the dark are already being exposed. Mankind is already starting an ascension process!

This is one reason why many are seeking the wisdom of THE EMERALD TABLETS at this time! Mankind is indeed striving to put together older Wisdom, with the new rays of Light even now flooding the planet.

Darkness has NEVER had total control over the Light. Just one spark of Light can obliterate much darkness… by at least a ten-to-one ratio!

As humanity begins to realize the tremendous power of their heart-light, the veils will be torn asunder and the Light will have full sway!

Know this: there are varying shades of darkness… and there are varying shades of Light. This is a time of choices. You may choose to move MORE towards the Light… or move MORE towards the dark!

Which feels better to your heart?

You can NEVER squash the desire in your heart for more Light, more Love, and even more Service!

Humans are programmed to seek the satisfaction of the heart. All else is futile and temporary… and will NOT bring that Soul's satisfaction!

Without heart and Soul satisfaction - there is no true and deep happiness. Life will seem empty and dull… no matter the outward appearance. Never, ever, turn your back on the power of your heart!

Meditation: Find the audio version of this at: https://www.eftexpert.com/blog/heart-power

This guided meditation will help you discover the power and Wisdom of your heart. Your heart's desires hold a significance you may not fully realize. This meditation is an anointing of the Holy Spirit, a message exactly tailored to what your heart needs to hear.

Close your eyes.

Let it be easy. As you close your eyes, start by relaxing the muscles in your head. Let go of any tension in your neck and shoulders, allowing the relaxation to flow softly down your arms, and into your hands.

Now, shift your awareness to your chest, gently placing your hand over your heart. Take a moment to appreciate the steady beat of your physical heart. Feel the gratitude for this rhythm of life.

As you continue to relax, release all tension in your back, your hips, your legs, and your feet. Allow each muscle to soften.

In this state of deep relaxation, imagine yourself as tiny, tiny, tiny. You are journeying downward from the crown of your head, through the cranial cavity, in awe of the intricate cranial activities.

Picture yourself arriving at your heart. In this tiny form, your heart appears enormous and majestic. You are an observer within your own being, gazing upon your heart.

With each beat of your heart, particles of light radiate out into the universe. Your heart contains a brilliant, glowing jewel within it. On the walls of your heart, there is Sacred language, inscribed in a code that is beyond your current understanding.

Remember, before you entered this physical existence… you made plans, you held desires. These are written on the walls of your heart, waiting to be revealed. As the power of the Holy Spirit descends upon these words, you begin to resonate and vibrate at a higher frequency.

Sacred language rolls off your tongue, moving out into the universe, expressing desires that are yet to come into being. These desires flow from your heart… like a stream of champagne, sparkling and effervescent.

Your heart swells with the music of your desires. With each breath, your heart's tuning becomes brighter and more magnetic. Now, it sends out Light vibrations in all directions.

Realize that every desire within your heart is a Sacred mission from the Divine - an agreement with your Higher Self to manifest these desires during this existence. Witness the majesty of your beating heart, and let its Wisdom speak to your physical ears.

Your heart is healing through this loving attention, growing more powerful. Breathe in the anointing of the Holy Spirit, expanding your capacity to Love, to show kindness and compassion, and to understand the importance of your mission on Earth at this time.

As you relax, feel yourself held in the loving embrace of your own heart. Express gratitude for its magnificence, for carrying you forward on this journey.

Now, imagine that you have a little microscope, and you're examining one of those desires, perhaps a desire you've been too afraid to speak aloud. Speak it now, breathe life into it. The more you claim it, the more magnetic it becomes… until it becomes your reality.

It's time to return to your consciousness, carrying the joy and Wisdom of your heart with you. As you come back to the present moment, appreciate the depth of your journey.

You now find yourself outside of your heart, filled with Love and appreciation for the Wisdom within. Allow this Love and appreciation to flow like music through your being.

If you feel that someone else would be uplifted or blessed by this meditation, please pass it on. Share the Love.

In closing, remember the words of the Divine Mother: "You can do no wrong in my eyes. You can do no wrong in my eyes. You can do no wrong in my eyes." Embrace this truth as your own. You can do no wrong in the eyes of the Divine.

NOTES AND QUESTIONS

Chapter Fourteen

TABLET 6, VERSE 14.
GUIDES OF THE ETERNAL WAY

Even as exist among men the DARK BROTHERS,
so there exist the BROTHERS of LIGHT.

Antagonists they of the BROTHERS of DARKNESS,
seeking to free men from the night.

Powers have they, mighty and potent.
Knowing the LAW, the planets obey.

Work they ever in harmony and order,
freeing the man-soul from its bondage of night.

Secret and hidden, walk they also.
Known not are they to the children of men.

Yet know that ever they walk with thee,
Showing the WAY to the children of men.

Thoth's Insight in Plain Language:

Just as there are dark beings who seek to gain the ultimate prize - the turning of a heart towards the dark... so there are also many beings of Light seeking to educate and protect the hearts of mankind.

This is an age-old struggle, and many of humankind are blinded to BOTH sides of this struggle. Many assume that they are here all alone, being neither aware of the dark brothers who seek to manipulate, nor the Light Beings who seek to educate and protect.

You may think it strange that I, Thoth, use the word educate. Yet, it is the education, and what is going on in the Spirit world, that will make your path more clear!

Be aware that there is both dark and Light. It could not be otherwise!

Just as the sun sets, and the dark creeps across the sky... so it is within all realms. Notice that even in the darkest of nights, there are still tiny pinpoints of Light twinkling in the sky!

It is time for humanity to fully awaken to the power which they have, to ALWAYS choose the LIGHT!

The dark will never have enough power to strangle out the Light. Just one tiny pinprick of Light will be enough to blast through layers of darkness and chaos.

You have the power of free will to always be alert, and choose the Light. This is NOT to cause any fear among you… rather to cause peace and a return to seeking Love and joy!

There is NO NEED to ever fear, when you KNOW that you have free will to always choose the Light-filled way! Respect the free will that you have, honor the heart that is so precious, and visualize your heart-light growing ever brighter. You have NAUGHT to fear.

These words are meant as a source of comfort to you. For have you not already been fearing to be overtaken by dark thoughts? Have you not already been believing that many others are so turned towards darkness that this world could not be saved?

Comfort ye, my precious ones! It is in education and awareness that triumph lives!

Meditation to Increase the Light in Your Heart
Enjoy the audio of this meditation:
https://www.eftexpert.com/blog/heart-light

This meditation will increase the Light in your heart, affecting your heart chakra and positively influencing all of your body systems.

This will assist you in your desire to perceive things in the Light, and to know that you have the power to always choose the Light. And so, relax. Everything works so much better when you're relaxed.

Relax the muscles in your head. Relax the muscles in your neck. And now, let your shoulders relax. Doesn't it feel good to just relax? Relax the muscles in your back, and now your chest. Relax the muscles in your abdomen as you slowly take in deep, slow breaths. Relax.

Let that relaxation now flow downward through your lower abdomen, the front of your legs, your kneecaps. Relax. Now your calves, and then the back of your body, all of your back muscles, relax. Now the hip muscles relax, the back of your legs, the back of your kneecaps, all the way down to your ankles, your toes, and especially the arches of your feet.

And now... our goal is to increase the Light in your heart, which will help you, not only, to be a beacon of Light for others... but also to be a beacon of Light for your own understanding. To facilitate this increase of Light, I am guided to focus on a part of the heart that you've probably never thought about - the pericardium. This is a thin membrane, like a protective sac, that surrounds the heart, and is filled with cushioning fluid.

When your heart feels heavy or broken, when you've suffered a lot of heartbreak, or when you're experiencing illness... this fluid can become cloudy.

It's our desire to perform an exchange of this fluid, that will fill your heart with Lightness, gladness, and Divine Light. It will begin to pump through the heart... then pump this Light-filled essence throughout your entire body.

How filled with Light do you feel right now? On a scale of one to ten - ten would be, "Oh, I'm so full of Light." Anything below five would be, "Oh, I need more Light in my heart. I need more Light in my entire body."

And so, imagine, if you will, there are two theoretical syringes that only slightly penetrate the pericardium. One syringe is a withdrawing device, and the other is an infilling device. It's very important that this fluid be maintained in balance at all times.

And so, as the first syringe begins to slowly withdraw the cloudy fluid, the other syringe begins to inject the pericardium with the Divine Light-filled fluid, simultaneously, in perfect harmony.

The most Sacred Light that is known, is the clear Light of Holy Spirit. When this clear Holy Spirit Light enters the human body, it indeed becomes as holy water. And as you can see with your Spiritual eye, this holy water fluid is filled with beautiful Light particles. It twinkles and dances... and almost tickles your heart.

And now, the exchange is complete. The withdrawing syringe is put away, and so is the infusing one. The pericardium is completely mended now, and the fluid surrounding your heart is singing the praises of the Light.

You know, beloved, when you don't know to whom to pray, or what to think, you can always call on the Light. I find great value and comfort in calling on the Light source, known as the Holy Spirit.

And, I have found that you can use the Light source of the Holy Spirit… as great healing. And so, if you would allow this great healing energy to permeate your pericardium, it would cushion you from the harsh realities of life.

Imagine now, that a few particles of this Light-filled fluid are entering into the actual heart wall. Every cell in your heart begins to replicate with the magical, effervescent glory of the Holy Spirit.

And now, those tiny particles enter your bloodstream. As you take a deep breath in and say, "Yes, fill me with the anointing of Holy Spirit," you will find that surges of Holy Spirit healing energy rush throughout your body, via the bloodstream. They trickle down into the depths within, until every part of your being is alive… tingling, glowing, healing, and loving the power of this Holy Spirit Light.

Allow yourself to continue to relax as long as you desire.

NOTES AND QUESTIONS

Chapter Fifteen

TABLET 6, VERSE 15.
ETERNAL VICTORY OF LIGHT

Ever have THEY fought the DARK BROTHERS,
conquered and conquering time without end.

Yet always LIGHT shall in the end be master,
driving away the darkness of night.

Aye, man, know ye this knowing:
always beside thee walk the Children of Light.

Thoth's Insight in Plain Language:

No need to fear being overtaken by the dark, as long as you realize the ongoing and ever-growing power of the Light! Light Beings are in the ether - walking beside you constantly!

They cannot, and will not, invade human free will. Yet, they seek for you to fully realize that they are there, and willing to serve!

Begin to consciously take heed and guidance from these Beings of Light, and you will see wondrous changes in your lifetime!

To discover just HOW these Beings of Light can help you… focus on your own beam of Source-Light within your heart. Imagine that you are pointing your strong beam of Holy Light directly into the face of the Light Being.

If the Being stands firm… he is of the Light.

A dark being cannot stay in the presence of a human heart-beam connected to Source. You can then begin communicating with the Light Beings all around you! As you practice this, you will become aware of wondrous acquaintances.

Just as YOU desire to serve humanity, so the Light Beings desire to serve! Being in service as a team, adds far more pleasure and ease in your journey! Imagine the comfort of always knowing that you have a team on your side.

NOTES AND QUESTIONS

Chapter Sixteen

TABLET 6, VERSE 16.
LORDS OF THE MORNING SUN

Masters they of the SUN power,
ever unseen yet the guardians of men.

Open to all is their pathway,
open to he who will walk in the LIGHT.

Free are THEY of DARK AMENTI,
free of the HALLS, where LIFE reigns supreme.

SUNS are they and LORDS of the morning,
Children of Light to shine among men.

Like man are they and yet are unlike,
Never divided were they in the past.

ONE have they been in ONENESS eternal,
throughout all space since the beginning of time.

Up did they come in Oneness with the ALL ONE,
up from the first-space, formed and unformed.

Thoth's Insight in Plain Language:

Again, we speak of the Beings of Light among you - Beings who have NEVER danced with the darkness. These Beings were created from Source to always carry the Light!

What a safe place to form a connection for the purpose of service! Every human feels the call of service, for it is their soul path to realize this! There is no joy greater than when you are serving in, or walking in, your heart and soul's purpose and path.

Many are always questioning… what is my purpose?

Your purpose has many facets. The greatest indicator is the joy you feel as you think about, or participate in, a certain activity. It is NOT hard, as many suppose, to find your purpose… follow the path that leads to more joy!

The Creator would NOT place you here in this realm, to have a purpose that is distasteful to you! Yes, it is that simple! Take baby steps toward finding more joy!

Part of the wonder of life is discovering joy along the way. A full blueprint of your life is never revealed.

Although, a full blueprint of your highest possibilities is indeed written on the walls of your heart.

This is one reason why you are always encouraged to tune in to your heart, and TRUST the guidance that you find there. Begin with small steps… and then larger ones. When a new phase of your purpose is unfolding, you may need to revert back to the baby step phase. All is growth!

NOTES AND QUESTIONS

Chapter Seventeen

TABLET 6, VERSE 17.
PATHS OF THE UNBOUND MASTER

Given to man have they secrets
that shall guard and protect him from all harm.

He who would travel the path of a master,
free must he be from the bondage of night.

Thoth's Insight in Plain Language:
Again, speaking of the powers of the Beings of Light who walk among you. Some call them Angels - some call them by other names. These Beings are different from what you know as Spirit Guides, for Spirit Guides have often been in human form.

To be in human form… means that there has been exposure to the dark brothers at some point of human existence.

The Beings we speak of now, have never been tempted by the darkness! They were created of Light, and have never wavered. Being in communion with these Beings of Light, will open the doors for the secrets to be revealed to you!

Ask for the secrets that will keep you from harm, and always in perfect safety, to be revealed to you! It is now time for that which has been hidden, to be made known. You have come far in your evolution and are ready to know, and to be trusted, with many secrets.

NOTES AND QUESTIONS

Chapter Eighteen

TABLET 6, VERSE 18.
CONQUERING THE PHANTOM OF FEAR

Conquer must he the formless and shapeless,
conquer must he the phantom of fear.

Knowing, must he gain of all of the secrets,
travel the pathway that leads through the darkness,
yet ever before him keep the light of his goal.

Obstacles great shall he meet in the pathway,
yet press on to the LIGHT of the SUN.

Thoth's Insight in Plain Language:

It is not enough just to think positive, while yes, that is one tool against the dark thoughts, it is but a beginning. Knowing that there are temptations to be seduced by the fake promises of the dark is brilliance. What you know about…you are on the alert for!

Recognizing that you DO have the help of the Light Beings who also walk beside you is a great positive force!

These Light Beings are just waiting for you to ask for assistance. I have said that they walk among you unannounced, yet when you RECOGNIZE that they are there…you have the connection needed to ask for assistance.

Your acknowledgement tears away the veil that has been obscuring your consciousness from connecting with this great source of help.

Better it is for you to create an active partnership with these Light Beings Than to remain in cluelessness.

Help is here for you, and it takes you in great strides forward on your spiritual journey to partner with the unseen forces of Light!

NOTES AND QUESTIONS

Chapter Nineteen

TABLET 6, VERSE 19.
THE BATTLE WITHIN THE MIND

Hear ye, O man, the SUN is the symbol
of the LIGHT that shines at the end of thy road.

Now to thee give I the secrets:
now to meet the dark power,
meet and conquer the fear from the night.

Only by knowing can ye conquer,
Only by knowing can ye have LIGHT.

Thoth's Insight in Plain Language:
It is true that there is a real force of darkness. Yet, much of the power that the darkness holds is simply in the mind of humans. Beings of Light see the fear energy you expend when thinking of encountering any dark power.

Yes, acknowledge that there may be temptations offered by the dark. Yet, the wise will simply recognize darkness for what it is. Theirs is a losing battle. **The battleground for you is between your ears.**

You may think that I am speaking much about the dark brothers here, yet I am speaking MORE about the importance of the Light!

Even if you simply close your eyes and IMAGINE your body being filled with Light… this is a powerful deterrent to the temptations of the dark.
You see, humans have failings around temptations.

They are sometimes lured into taking shortcuts to power, by the frequency of greed.

Humanity is deeply programmed to be in survival mode. This can make it easy for people to fall prey to any promise of elevation by nefarious means.

It is your birthright to be abundant! You have been lied to, and programmed, to think that abundance is only for a few. Worse, many are thinking that to have much wealth, requires you to turn to dark ways.

As you realize that wealth can be obtained with more ease, and as you give yourself permission to believe that you are already WORTHY… much advancement shall occur!

You have simply been in a rut - thinking that wealth can only be gotten through stealthy ways. This has robbed you of your right inheritance!

The road to greater abundance begins with forgiveness and pardon. Forgive those who programmed you. Forgive the patterns of poverty.

Follow this advice, and you will begin to thrive! You will automatically be aware - and open to - your next best step forward.

NOTES AND QUESTIONS

Chapter Twenty

TABLET 6, VERSE 20.
THE CONQUERING WISDOM

Now I give unto thee the knowledge,
known to the MASTERS,
the knowing that conquers all the dark fears.

Use this, the wisdom I give thee.
MASTERS thou shalt be of the BROTHERS of NIGHT.

Thoth's Insight in Plain Language:

Pay heed to all that I have said. Keep your focus on the Light!

Know that you are worthy of all good. Ask for help from the Light Beings who are already walking with you.

NOTES AND QUESTIONS

Chapter Twenty-one

TABLET 6, VERSE 21.
GUARDING THE MIND'S GATE

When unto thee there comes a feeling,
drawing thee nearer to the dark gate,
examine thine heart and find if the feeling
thou hast has come from within.

If thou shalt find the darkness thine own thoughts,
banish them forth from the place in thy mind.

Send through thy body a wave of vibration,
irregular first and regular second,
repeating time after time until free.

Start the WAVE FORCE in thy BRAIN CENTER.
Direct it in waves from thine head to thy foot.

Thoth's Insight in Plain Language:
If you find that you are having dark thoughts -
thoughts of failure or thoughts of suicide - know that

a particle of darkness has penetrated into your mind. You are NOT overtaken… it is simply an *oppression.

Yet, do not let this oppression take you over! This is how people go "off the deep end," and do harmful things… harmful to their own body or harmful to others.

(*Another word for oppression is feeling overly pressured.)

It is in the spirit of desperation that true failure occurs. Pay attention, BANISH these thoughts from your brain.

Yes, use the WORDS OF BANISHMENT!
CHEQUETET (Phonetic Pronunciation ~ CHE-KWET-TET)
ARELICH (Phonetic Pronunciation ~ AR-LICK)
VOMALITES (Phonetic Pronunciation ~ VO-MAL-E-TESS)

Do not fear that you will seem foolish. This is your own life that you are saving!

Draw in Sacred Light from the space above your head! Draw it through the Pineal gland… then down through the thalamus system, pituitary gland, and clean the entire brain.

Imagine alternating waves of this Sacred Light…
flooding first your brain, and then down your body.
Imagine it as a wave form - first vibrating in an irregular rhythm, then alternating with a regular rhythm.

Use the power of your breath to regulate this. Do this thirty-six times. You are taking ACTION to dislodge all remnants.

NOTES AND QUESTIONS

Chapter Twenty-two

TABLET 6, VERSE 22.
THE POWER OF KNOWING

But if thou findest thine heart is not darkened,
be sure that a force is directed to thee.

Only by knowing can thou overcome it.
Only by wisdom can thou hope to be free.

Knowledge brings wisdom and wisdom is power.
Attain and ye shall have power o'er all.

Thoth's Insight in Plain Language:

It is the purpose of the dark brothers to be an interference to those who are effectively turning others to the Light, and more closely following the path of Goodness and Light themselves.

It is a GOOD sign that you are standing out as a Lightworker!

It is simply another step forward to be aware, and to KNOW, that there is an easy solution. Being aware of when you are under psychic attack, and taking steps to STOP it in its tracks, is key to your forward movement.

We see that many may feel a sense of fear as they read these words. To us, it is simply part of the journey. Do not think that the dark brothers approach you openly. No, they present as some type of obstacle.

It is important to "tune in," and to know when spiritual intervention is needed… or if the obstacle is simply a circumstance attributed to normal situations.

The Ritual in the next chapter will be beneficial to your energy centers, whether you are under attack or not. It will balance and harmonize all of your body systems!

NOTES AND QUESTIONS

Chapter Twenty-three

TABLET 6, VERSE 23.
RITUAL OF LIBERATION

Seek ye first a place bound with darkness.
Place ye a circle around about thee.

Stand erect in the midst of the circle.
Use thou this formula, and thou shalt be free.

Raise thou thine hands to the dark space above thee.
Close thou thine eyes and draw in the LIGHT.

Call to the SPIRIT OF LIGHT through the Space-Time,
using these words and thou shalt be free:
"Fill thou my body, O SPIRIT OF LIFE,
fill thou my body with SPIRIT OF LIGHT.

Come from the FLOWER
that shines through the darkness.

Come from the HALLS where the Seven Lords rule.
Name them by name, I, the Seven:
THREE, FOUR, FIVE,
and SIX, SEVEN, EIGHT-NINE.

Thoth's Insight in Plain Language:

This is part one of a two-step Ritual to eradicate any darkness from your energy space. Follow these instructions. Then use the words below. This will empower you... and dense energies will flee.

They will find it impossible to remain in your energy! The frequency created by these powerful names, spoken with authority, causes a balance and harmony, such as is only possible by attuning yourself to these Sacred words.

Words have power. They also possess a great sound signature which has been tuned into by many beings throughout the ages.

These power words below - in the next chapter - have been used by other species of Starbrothers to strengthen their energy fields. Your earth realm is NOT the only realm or dimension that is seeking the Light.

Other species also have a soul purpose and face the same challenges that you do... perhaps presented in a different time and space.

NOTES AND QUESTIONS

Chapter Twenty-four

TABLET 6, VERSE 24.
CHANT OF THE SEVEN LORDS

By their names, I call them to aid me,
free me and save me from the darkness of night:
UNTANAS, QUERTAS, CHIETAL,
and GOYANA, HUERTAL, SEMVETA, ARDAL.

By their names I implore thee,
free me from darkness
and fill me with LIGHT."

Thoth's Insight in Plain Language:

These names are actual "Beings of Frequency," dedicated to Light and balance! Chanting their names, even at random, will strengthen and balance your entire energy system!

The names correspond with the seven major chakras. It is good to imagine your heart connecting with each one of these seven Lords!

They are part of the Brothers of Light who walk among you. Call upon them as you will! Give them credit for the harmony you feel as you do this.

This is encouragement to them. To be acknowledged by those they are desiring to serve is a great blessing to them.

So also, is it a great blessing when you acknowledge the unseen Light Beings who also walk among you. It is a sign of your ascension when you are awake enough to be aware and in union with the unseen of the Light!

So much MORE of this realm is happening in the unseen. Tapping into the GOODNESS of it will surely encourage you, and lift your frequencies to the stars!

NOTES AND QUESTIONS

Chapter Twenty-five

TABLET 6, VERSE 25.
THE POWER OF SACRED NAMES

Know ye, O man, that when ye have done this,
ye shall be free from the fetters that bind ye,
cast off the bondage of the BROTHERS of NIGHT.

See ye not that the names have the power
to free by vibration the fetters that bind?

Use them at need to free thou thine brother
so that he, too, may come forth from the night.

Thoth's Insight in Plain Language:
This simple Ritual will set you free from any oppressive energies which you may be feeling. Although it is simple, the frequencies are very powerful!

After chanting for yourself, it is good to think of a person who also needs some freedom from bondage.

Hold that person in your heart as you do the Ritual again on their behalf.

Of course, you do not overpower human will... they will accept or reject the release you are intending. However; if they are in a sad state because they are OPPRESSED, this act will diminish the oppressive forces so that they have more access to their own free will.

Sometimes a person is so surrounded by the dense energies that they need Spiritual help - yes, intervention, to be able to regain their power. It is important to pay attention to the promptings of your heart, for your heart KNOWS when to help and when to hold back.

Never override the wisdom and guidance of your heart!

NOTES AND QUESTIONS

Chapter Twenty-six

TABLET 6, VERSE 26.
LIFT THY BROTHER FROM NIGHT

Thou, O man, art thy brother's helper.
Let him not lie in the bondage of night.

Thoth's Insight in Plain Language:

Yes, you are indeed a helper of all. Yet, only when moved upon by the Spirit of Light. As you become more Spiritually aware, you will be able to discern who to help, and who is not ready to receive help.

Having the GOOD intentions to be open to the promptings of your heart, will make life much more simple for you. Many feel the burdens of the whole world, and it weighs heavily on them.

This can lead to a feeling of helplessness… as you feel that ONE person could not make a difference.

Brothers and sisters, you are only called to make that difference when guided! The more you attune to your heart's promptings, the more you will KNOW. Your burden of concern for others will be a guiding force, only when it is part of YOUR job.

Always trust your heart's guidance!

Feeling TOO much concern when it is NOT your soul's purpose to help with a certain thing, is actually an ego-driven concern. It leads to feelings of overwhelm and helplessness.

The more you attune to your heart's guidance, the more clear your mission will become.

If it is NOT your path to help with a certain cause, it is good for you to pray for that cause to be addressed by the perfect match to bring the solution.

You can do so much more good than you realize, by turning loose of your guilt over circumstances that are not yours to address.

NOTES AND QUESTIONS

Chapter Twenty-seven

TABLET 6, VERSE 27.
ASCEND WITH MY WORDS

Now unto thee, give I my magic.
Take it and dwell on the pathway of LIGHT.

Thoth's Insight in Plain Language:

My Magic is the words I speak… the guidance I give. I see you ascending higher and higher into the realms of Light. It is more simple than you know.

I have been addressing the importance of tuning into your heart and trusting the guidance there… This is the way of truth. Do this and you have nothing to fear.

NOTES AND QUESTIONS

Chapter Twenty-eight

TABLET 6, VERSE 28.
THE PATH OF PEACE AND POWER

LIGHT unto thee, LIFE unto thee,
SUN may thou be on the cycle above.

Thoth's Insight in Plain Language:

Take this Blessing which I give to you. It is not by chance that you are reading these words. Know that you have chosen to be on this path. Know that there is much good for you here, and much good that you can do for this world.

Peace be with you. Always turn within, and always trust your heart.

Balance yourself often by calling on the seven Lords of Frequency. UNTANAS, QUERTAS, CHIETAL, and GOYANA, HUERTAL, SEMVETA, ARDAL.

These are referring as well, to the seven seals, or chakras. Tap on each chakra center as you say each name of the Lord of Frequency.

UNTANAS ~ Crown Chakra
QUERTAS ~ Third Eye Chakra
CHIETAL ~ Throat Chakra
GOYANA ~ Heart Chakra
HUERTAL ~ Solar Plexus Chakra
SEMVETA ~ Sexual Chakra
ARDAL ~ Root Chakra

NOTES AND QUESTIONS

Chapter Twenty-Nine

FINAL THOUGHTS

It is my heartfelt hope that you practice some of the exercises you've just read. Naturally, some may come easier to you than others.

Personally, I find great comfort and strength in calling out the names of the Seven Lords, while tapping on each chakra that they represent.

In fact, I've even written their names on my coffee pot, so that I see them every morning!

Remember this: as you follow the wisdom of Thoth the Atlantean, your life will improve, and your Spirit will soar!

Most importantly, trust that the wisdom of your own heart is your TRUE guiding system.

I've always believed that the Divine sent us here with everything we need, already written on the walls of our hearts!

It would be a true joy to hear from you, and to know how you're doing on your journey. Feel free to reach out to me (and to Thoth) at Rebecca@rebeccamarina.com.

Chapter Thirty

ABOUT THE AUTHOR

Rebecca Marina Messenger is a world-renowned Spiritual teacher, author, and healer - with more than three decades of experience channeling Divine messages, and guiding others on their Spiritual journeys. After a life-changing encounter with Archangel Gabriel, Rebecca's psychic abilities became awakened, opening the door for daily communication with countless Beings of Light!

As the Founder and Mastermind of Celebration Healing, Rebecca has reached more than two million people worldwide… through her online platforms, workshops, TikTok, YouTube, and EFT (Emotional Freedom Technique) certification classes. In addition, she channeled information from Divine Mother, in order to bring HPT (Heart Point Technique) to the world - an amazing and powerful healing modality.

Known for her joyful, motherly energy - and her powerful connection to Light Beings and the Divine

- she offers profound teachings on Spirituality, healing trauma, and psychic development. Her dazzling insights often bring amazing healing to many around the world!

Rebecca's expertise spans a range of modalities, including mediumship, EFT, channeling, and heart-centered coaching. Her intuitive insights into past-life issues, and physical, emotional, and Spiritual healing, are constantly sought-after by clients from all walks of life, including experienced healers.

Rebecca's work is driven by her deep passion to help others to unlock their highest potential, and to live joyfully. She continually empowers her clients and readers. She helps them to hold a clear vision of their desires, release their inner obstacles, and illuminate their Divine path ahead. Many times, she has been instrumental in providing the assistance needed for people to realize the long-held desires of their hearts.

Rebecca resides in Texas with her husband - where they enjoy dancing and living life to the fullest. They have two very feisty chihuahuas, who bring joy and entertainment into the house.

Rebecca is dedicated to constantly expanding her reach, in order to help more people to discover and develop their Spiritual gifts. She is most proud to remain intimately connected daily to all of her five - now adult - children.

This amazing, heart-centered Lady cares about all beings so deeply, that she feeds all of the neighborhood cats, possums, birds, fish, and more! She, also, daily rescues other critters found in her yard needing help.

Rebecca is an amazing Spiritual Guide, Divine Whisperer, and Compassionate Soul! She's like a Spiritual GPS, who is skilled at helping you to "recalculate" when needed, so that you are able to find your Spiritual path joyfully.

Printed in the USA
CPSIA information can be obtained
at www.ICGtesting.com
LVHW010744081124
795954LV00021B/381